Cheetah Dreams

by Linda Stanek
illustrated by Shennen Bersani

I dream of cheetahs
racing on
across the bright savanna.

The cheetah is the fastest land animal. Cheetahs can run up to seventy miles (113 km) per hour, going from zero to sixty in just three seconds. It's exhausting! Luckily, most of the time, cheetahs are able to catch their prey at only half that speed.

Unlike other big cats in Africa, cheetahs are most active during the day (diurnal).

Their cleat-like feet
    so swift and sure,
their tails like rudders,
    guiding.

Like the nubby cleats on the bottom of athletic shoes, cheetahs' claws are always partly out, ready to grip the ground as the big cat runs.

Cheetahs use their tails like the rudder of a boat. Their tails help them to balance and steer their bodies when they turn at high speeds.

I dream of cheetahs
safe, secure,
from farmers strictly guarding.

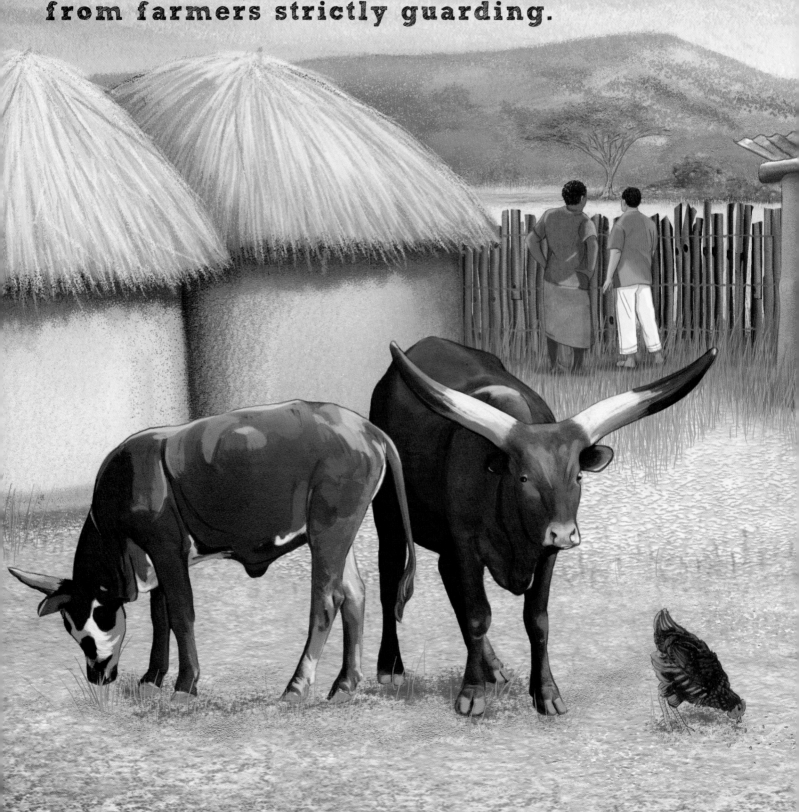

When farmers move into cheetah territory, the cheetahs' preferred prey, gazelle and young wildebeest, move away. But cheetahs still need food. Some of them end up hunting the livestock on farms.

To protect their livestock, these farmers sometimes resort to shooting the cheetahs.

Of dogs with voices,
      deep and loud,
to urge the cheetahs onward.

Some farms have large, loud, Anatolian shepherd dogs that live with the farm animals. When these dogs sense a cheetah nearby, they bark and growl.

Cheetahs are better at running than fighting, so when they hear the dogs, they take off. These dogs save the livestock from the cheetahs, and the cheetahs from farmers.

I dream of cheetahs'
amber eyes,

their tear-marked faces **watching**;

Cheetahs have malar stripes, or "tear marks," made of black fur that runs from their eyes to their mouths. Less sunshine reflects off this black fur and into cheetahs' eyes.

their listening, black
and tawny ears
that guide the
cheetahs' hunting.

Cheetahs have excellent hearing, and their ears help in other ways too. Black blotches of fur on the backs of their ears might look like eyes to an animal creeping up from behind. The dark fur also makes it easier for cheetah cubs to keep track of their mother when they follow her.

I dream of cheetahs'
tiny cubs,
their high-pitched voices
chirping,

Cheetahs generally have three to five babies in each litter. Cubs make a chirping sound when they cry out.

When cubs are very young, their mother must leave them behind while she hunts. This is an especially dangerous time for baby cheetahs.

of mothers moving
here and there,
to keep their babies **hiding**.

To keep their babies from being found by predators, mother cheetahs move their cubs to a new den about every three days. When babies are about two months old, they begin following their mother as she hunts.

Cubs stay with their mother for almost two years before they are on their own.

I dream of cheetahs'

bellies full,
of young ones
strong and growing,

Cheetahs are built for racing, but running at top speed exhausts them, so they sometimes need to rest for up to thirty minutes afterward.

About half the time, another animal—a lion, leopard, hyena, or even vultures—will take advantage of this and steal a cheetah's kill, leaving the exhausted animal without food.

of tracts of land
        where cheetahs stand
and **wander** through the wilds.

When cheetahs lose land to humans, they not only have fewer places to live, but they are sometimes cut off from other cheetahs. We call this "fragmented territory."

Fragmented territory makes it difficult for cheetahs to find mates. And traveling through human-populated areas is dangerous. This can result in more adult cheetahs dying, and fewer babies.

I dream of deep and
rumbling sounds,
of cheetahs softly purring.

Unlike other big cats (like lions, tigers, jaguars, and leopards), cheetahs cannot roar. Cheetahs make many sounds, including chirping, snarling, hissing, and growling. And unlike their roaring cousins, cheetahs can purr when they are happy.

I dream of cheetahs
racing on . . .

Of all the wild cats in Africa, cheetahs' numbers are dropping the fastest. People worry that they could become extinct. But you can help by spreading the word that cheetahs need our help.

After all, finding a solution to any problem begins with letting others know that there is a problem.

. . . extinction far behind them.

For Creative Minds

Cheetahs and their Big Cat Cousins

Cats come in all sizes, from the rusty-spotted cat (2-3.5 lb or 9-1.6 kg) to the Siberian tiger (up to 675 lb or 306 kg). Some cat species are grouped together and called the "big cats." Lions, tigers, leopards, and jaguars are all big cats. Sometimes other cats, like cheetahs, pumas, and snow leopards, are called big cats too.

Cheetahs are smaller than their big cat cousins, but they are still pretty big! An adult cheetah is 3.5 to 4.5 feet (1.1-1.4 m) long from its head to the base of its tail. The tail adds another 2 to 2.5 feet (.6 to .76 m). Cheetahs are about 32 inches (.8 m) tall at their shoulders, and weigh 70-140 lb. (32-64 kg).

From left to right: human, lion, jaguar, cheetah, house cat, leopard, tiger.

Which of these are not "Big Cats"?

Cheetah Conservation

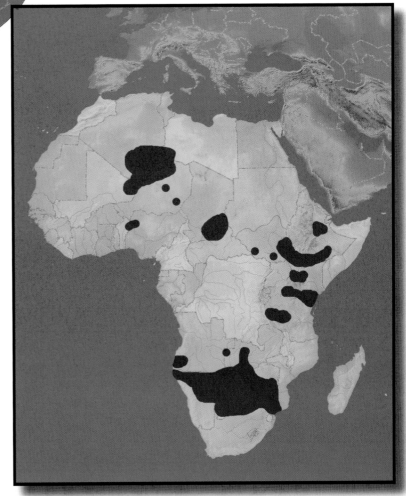

There are 54 different countries on the continent of Africa . . . and cheetahs used to live in nearly all of them, and on other continents too! But not anymore—now cheetahs live only in the areas shown on this map.

Only one in ten cheetah cubs survives to adulthood. Some die from health problems when they are young. Many cubs are killed by predators such as lions or hyenas. This can happen when the mother cheetah is out hunting, or even when she is with her cubs. She is not big and strong enough to fight off either of these predators.

Once a cheetah reaches adulthood, it faces new challenges. Fragmented territory makes it hard for cheetahs to move around in their habitat. Farms and human populations make the cheetahs' territories smaller and smaller. People hunt many of the same prey cheetahs do, so there are fewer prey animals left for the cheetahs. And some people hunt cheetahs too. In most countries, this is illegal and is called poaching.

What are we doing?

As with most endangered species, education is a big part of conservation. Zoos and conservation organizations teach people about the threats to cheetahs. They raise money to create wildlife refuges where cheetahs will be safe from poachers and away from farms. About 10% of wild cheetahs live in these protected areas. Some zoos are working on captive breeding programs, so that the cheetahs in their zoos can have babies and help the global population.

Cheetah Adaptations

Cheetahs have larger than normal hearts and lungs for an animal of their size. Their extra-large lungs allow them to take in plenty of oxygen, and their big hearts pump the oxygen through their bodies, fueling them when they run at top speed.

Cheetahs' claws are adapted to help them run. While most cats' claws withdraw into their paws (retractable claws) cheetahs' claws are only partially retractable. They are always ready to grip the ground, much like the cleats on athletic shoes.

Cheetahs' large eyes are set high in their skulls and face forward. This, along with the shape of their retinas (a part of the eye), gives them binocular vision. Cheetahs can see details of things more than three miles away.

Young cheetahs grow a "mantle" of long hair on the tops of their heads, their necks, and their backs. Some believe this is to make them look like the honey badger, a fierce, small animal that most predators leave alone. Others believe the mantle is to help the cubs blend in with the grass.

Purr or Roar

Some cats purr. Other cats roar. But they can't do both. Why? Two reasons.

Every cat has a bone in its throat called the hyoid bone. In purring cats, this bone is hard and connects to other bones. It transmits vibrations when the cat purrs. In roaring cats, this bone is more flexible and it "floats"—it attaches to muscle, but not to other bones, so it doesn't transmit vibrations well.

The vocal cords of purring and roaring cats are also different. Vocal cords in purring cats fold in a special way that allows them to vibrate when the cat breathes in and out. Because of this, these cats can purr without stopping to catch their breath. The vocal cords in roaring cats are shaped differently. Their vocal cords, along with their floating hyoid bones, keep them from purring, but allow big cats to make loud, deep sounds. Roar! Some roaring cats can make something like a purring sound when they breathe out, but they have to stop to breathe in, so it isn't a true purr.

Do you think these cats have floating hyoid bones or attached? Why?

Lions use their deep, rolling **roar** to tell other lions where they are. This warns strange lions to stay away from the lion group (pride) that lives in the area.	Jaguars are the largest cats in the Americas. Unlike many other cats, jaguars like the water. They swim, hunt fish, bathe, and even play in the water. They have a deep **roar**.	Most animals freeze when they hear a tiger's **roar**. If the prey are scared stiff, they are easier for the tiger to catch!
Cheetahs are awake and active during the day. Sometimes they find a cool spot to rest during the hot afternoon, and stretch out to **purr** in the shade.	Leopards don't roar as loud as lions, or as long. Leopard **roars** are short and raspy, like the sound of a saw moving back-and-forth through wood.	House cats might live with people, but they haven't lost their wild, hunter instinct. Cats will hunt birds and small mammals, and then return home to curl up and **purr** in their favorite person's lap.

Floating hyoid bone (can roar): lion, jaguar, leopard, tiger. Attached hyoid bones (can purr): cheetah, house cat.

To Suzi Rapp and Shannon Swint with thanks for allowing me to step into your cheetah-filled world. Thanks, too, to Linda Castaneda, Alicia Sampson, Susie Ekard, and Janet Rose-Hinostroza for your insights on these amazing cats as well.—LS

To research these illustrations I drove to Southwick's Zoo in Mendon, MA, Roger Williams Park Zoo in Providence, RI, and Columbus Zoo in Columbus, Ohio, to see their cheetahs. I am truly grateful for Luke Weatherhead at Southwick's and Shannon Swint at Columbus for the time each of you spent with me, giving me access to your zoos' cheetahs, and answering my many questions. There is nothing quite like having the breath of a cheetah on your face. A special thank you to Lou Marcoccio for joining me on these zoo adventures.—SB

Thanks to Dr. Laurie Marker, Founder and Executive Director of the Cheetah Conservation Fund (CCF), and Suzi Rapp and Shannon Swint, VP and Office Coordinator of Animal Programs at Columbus Zoo, for verifying the accuracy of the information in this book.

Library of Congress Cataloging-in-Publication Data

Names: Stanek, Linda, author. | Bersani, Shennen, illustrator.
Title: Cheetah dreams / by Linda Stanek ; illustrated by Shennen Bersani.
Description: Mount Pleasant, SC : Arbordale Publishing, [2018] | Audience:
   Ages 4-8. | Audience: K to grade 3.
Identifiers: LCCN 2018005023 (print) | LCCN 2018005928 (ebook) | ISBN
   9781607187547 (English Downloadable eBook) | ISBN 9781607187660 (English
   Interactive Dual-Language eBook) | ISBN 9781607187592 (Spanish
   Downloadable eBook) | ISBN 9781607187714 (Spanish Interactive
   Dual-Language eBook) | ISBN 9781607187271 (english hardcover) | ISBN
   9781607187417 (english pbk.) | ISBN 9781607187479 (spanish pbk.)
Subjects: LCSH: Cheetah--Juvenile literature. | Cheetah--Behavior--Juvenile
   literature. | Endangered species--Africa--Juvenile literature.
Classification: LCC QL737.C23 (ebook) | LCC QL737.C23 S71645 2018 (print) |
   DDC 599.75/9--dc23
LC record available at https://lccn.loc.gov/2018005023

Bibliography

Becker, John. Frenemies for Life: Cheetahs and Anatolian Shepherd Dogs. Columbus: The Columbus Zoo and Aquarium, 2010. Print.
"Cheetah." Association of Zoos and Aquariums, 2016-2017. Web.
"Cheetah." National Geographic, 2017. Web.
Marker, Laurie, Lorraine K. Boast, Anne Schmidt-Kuentzel, Philip J. Nyhus (editors). Cheetahs: Biology and Conservation: Biodiversity of the World: Conservation from Genes to Landscapes. London: Academic Press, 2017. Print.
Rapp, Suzi. Personal interviews, 2016-17.
Sampson, Alicia. Email interview, June 9, 2017.

Lexile® Level: 710L
key phrases: critically endangered animals, habitat change, cheetahs, African animals, envirnomental education

Printed in China, July 2018
This product conforms to CPSIA 2008
First Printing

Arbordale Publishing
Mt. Pleasant, SC 29464
www.ArbordalePublishing.com